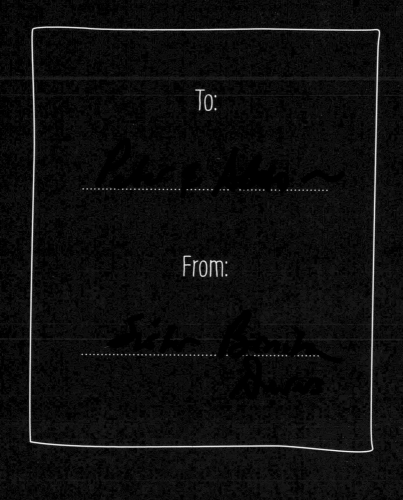

101 Secrets to a Happy Marriage

Real Couples Share the Keys to Their Success

with quotes by Harry Harrison

Thomas Nelson
Since 1798

NASHVILLE   MEXICO CITY   RIO DE JANEIRO

Published in Nashville, Tennessee, by Thomas Nelson. Thomas Nelson is a registered trademark of HarperCollins Christian Publishing, Inc.

Cover design by Connie Gabbert

Thomas Nelson titles may be purchased in bulk for educational, business, fund-raising, or sales promotional use. For information, please e-mail SpecialMarkets@ThomasNelson.com.

Unless otherwise noted, Scripture quotations are taken from The Holy Bible, New International Version®. Copyright © 1973, 1978, 1984, 2011 by Biblica, Inc.™ Used by permission. All rights reserved worldwide. www.zondervan.com. Scripture quotations marked NLT are taken from the *Holy Bible*, New Living Translation, copyright © 1996, 2004, 2007 by Tyndale House Foundation.. Used by permission of Tyndale House Publishers, Inc., Carol Stream, Illinois 60188. All rights reserved. Scripture quotations marked NKJV are taken from THE NEW KING JAMES VERSION. © 1982 by Thomas Nelson, Inc. Used by permission. All rights reverved. Scripture quotations marked HCSB are taken from the Holman Christian Standard Bible®, Copyright © 1999, 2000, 2002, 2003, 2009 by Holman Bible Publishers. Used by permission. Holman Christian Standard Bible®, Holman CSB®, and HCSB® are federally registered trademarks of Holman Bible Publishers.

Secret #49 was reprinted by permission. *Building Family Ties with Faith, Love & Laughter* by Dave Stone, copyright © 2012 by Thomas Nelson, Nashville, Tennessee. All rights reserved.
Secret #51 was reprinted by permission. *Total Money Makeover* by Dave Ramsey, copyright © 2003 by Thomas Nelson, Inc., Nashville, Tennessee. All rights reserved.
Secret #64 was reprinted by permission. *From My Heart to Yours* by Robin McGraw, copyright © 2009 by Thomas Nelson, Inc., Nashville, Tennessee. All rights reserved.
Secret #72 was taken from *Joy of a Sacred Marriage* by Gary Thomas. Copyright © 2007. Used by permission of Zondervan. www.zondervan.com
Secret #75 was reprinted by permission. *No Greater Love* by Russ Rice, Brad Silverman, and Lisa Guest, copyright © 2010 by Thomas Nelson, Inc., Nashville, Tennessee. All rights reserved.
Secret #88 was reprinted by permission. *Max on Life* by Max Lucado, copyright © 2010 by Thomas Nelson, Inc., Nashville, Tennessee. All rights reserved.
Secret #84 was reprinted by permission. *Man Stuff* by Josh Turner, copyright © 2013 by Thomas Nelson, Nashville, Tennessee. All rights reserved.
Secret #89 was reprinted by permission. *Building Family Ties with Faith, Love & Laughter* by Dave Stone, copyright © 2012 by Thomas Nelson, Nashville, Tennessee. All rights reserved.

ISBN-13: 978-0-7180-3048-3

Printed in China
17 18 19 20 DSC 6 5 4 3 2

www.thomasnelson.com

Every action and reaction we
share as husband and wife, every
moment we experience in marriage,
is a brushstroke of colorful paint
smeared across the canvas of life.

Jennifer Smith

The idea
is to marry your
best friend.

1. Always treat your partner with the utmost respect and love, the exact same way you would want to be treated by him or her.

—Charla & David Bennett, married 21 years

2. Before we were even married, we had discussed expectations, roles, convictions, money-handling principles, and child rearing. The communication that initiated our relationship has marked our entire marriage. We continue to make time to have heart-to-heart talks and pray together.

—Paul & Holly Brown, married 5 years

Don't be surprised if
after a few years of
wonderful, quiet nights
there is suddenly
snoring in your bed.
It may not be him.

3. Dr. Leslie Parrott says that until we are willing to do the hard work of becoming whole on our own, all our relationships will fall disappointingly flat. By allowing Christ to meet my emotional and spiritual needs, I have found inner peace and lasting joy that spills over into my marriage. Before I learned this nugget of wisdom, I wasted much energy on trying to get my husband to meet those needs, and you know what? It didn't work! I have learned to be intentional about the care of my body, mind, and spirit and have found that when I am whole, then my marriage is a blessing and a witness to those who are able to see what God can do in a marriage.

—Kolinda & Thomas Duer, married 27 years

•••••••••

4. The most important lessons I have learned are "choosing to constantly forgive" and "accepting my husband for who he is." Let go of all expectations and idealism and create together what only the two of you can—a wonderful life story that no one can re-create Pray for each other and appreciate your differences. Have plenty of adventurous morning, afternoon, or evening dates. Keep sexual intimacy interesting and spontaneous.

—Bergeman & Guirlene Jean, married 7 years

5. Four important words:
You may be right . . .

—Beth & Kirk Pulley, married 5 years

•••••••••

6. Kiss each other. Pick your battles. Remain committed. Cherish each day God gives you. Dance with happy feet. Encourage each other. Lavish each other with goodness. Honor each other. Remind your spouse how important he or she is to you. Journey through your married life as players on the same team. Never use the *D* word! Pursue each other passionately. Be self-sacrificing. Tell the truth always! Be understanding. Keep your marriage vows. Watch your words. Examine your motives when placing expectations on the other.

—Krystal & Bob Marusin, married 22 years

Your husband will not let go of
the remote control for one reason:
he doesn't trust you with it. As
long as he's holding it, there's
little chance of *House Hunters* or
Desperate Housewives suddenly
popping up on the screen.

A husband can look at a bedroom
and think it's perfectly fine. A wife
will look at it and think the sheets
need changing, clothes need to
be hung up, the carpet needs
vacuuming, the windows need
cleaning, and something needs to
be done with his shoes.

7. Prayer is the best way we have found to soften our hearts toward each other and to remain a unified team. We have set aside time once a week to get up early and pray. Often, when we begin, my heart is a bit hardened toward something or toward my husband. But by the end of prayer time, the Holy Spirit has entered and transformed that space. Not only does He take that hardness away, He draws us closer to each other. I am still surprised by it, though it happens without fail.

—Krista & Erik Gilbert, married 19 years

•••••••••

8. Decide early on that it is okay to disagree. When you discuss things, you will disagree, and that's okay. What's most important is that you remember how much you love each other, regardless of what you're discussing or disagreeing about.

—Richard & Stela Heuschkel, married 18 years

Thanks to the DVR, a man
doesn't have to miss a
moment of great TV just
because she wants to talk.
And then talk some more.
And then talk some more.

9. I think it's vital to choose the most important qualities (kindness, humor, a love of art/music) and then focus on those qualities when the other person seems like an alien creature (my unwillingness to drive freeways in the rain, his reluctance to throw away that unusable sliver of soap). Marriage is not about weird habits, food, sex, money, or which side we take regarding the death penalty. My husband is my biggest fan, and I'm his. We show true interest in each other's lives. He is the person I'm most loyal to, and the person I want to see first thing in the morning and last thing at night. His hand is the warmest and safest, and the only one I want to hold.

— Rusty & Tony Harris, married 22 years

•••••••••

10. We are all imperfect, so when you fight, fight productively. Don't let drama into a difficult discussion. Stick with what has really upset you, and think before you speak. Remember that the enemy's goal is to cause separation; don't let him in! God gave you your spouse to love no matter what. You can work through *anything*—yes, anything!

—Eric & Jill Slusher, married 10 years

If you find yourself
thinking your husband is
the weirdest person in
the world, ask yourself
who would be weird
enough to marry him.

•••••••

11. The secret to my happy marriage has been the fact that my husband and I always have each other's backs. Whether or not I agree with him or he with me, we stand united, especially in public, and then work out any differences or disagreements behind closed doors. That unconditional support is needed in a marriage for success and happiness.

—Joy Hill-Padilla & Joe Padilla,
married 14 years

•••••••

12. If you guard your heart and marriage from any one thing, let it be pride.

Pride is a wall that blocks intimacy with God and each other. If left unchecked, the poison of pride will leave both spouses out in the cold to fend for themselves against attacks from the enemy and hardship. However, if we fix our eyes on Jesus we see the ultimate example of love through humility. Jesus was God, but still He humbled himself . . . even to death on a cross—because He loves us. (Philippians 2)

Humility disarms tension, deflates the self, removes the unhealthy sense of self-importance, and places our primary concern on the other person. Humility reminds us that we desperately need grace, mercy, and forgiveness—and once we've truly experienced these, how can we not give them freely to each other?

By choosing humility, you choose love.

—Ryan & Selena Frederick, FierceMarriage.com,
married 12 years

Husbands who agree
with their wives are
90 percent more likely
to stay happily married.

13. It took a while, but finally I moved past the idea that you don't have to do things a particular way just because your folks, friends, or siblings do it that way. You have to make choices that work best for you as a couple. For example, I have a bigger chunk of time to tackle laundry and housework, so I don't expect my husband to do those things. We do our finances differently than others. We have a joint account we use for "big" things, in addition to our own separate accounts. We have had very few arguments about money in the last sixteen years together. I think people get caught up in how they think marriage should be, instead of focusing on what actually works best for the people involved.

—Keela & Michael Bryant,
married 14 years

When a husband does the laundry, whites, delicates, colors, bathroom rugs, and nightgowns all look the same to him. You have two choices: teach him to separate or never ask him to do the wash.

14. Be willing to support your spouse's dreams no matter how impossible they may seem. As companions and partners in life, we are not only called to love and respect our spouses, but also to allow them to become all that God wants them to be. If you support your spouse's dream and it fails, love your partner through the pain and disappointment. If you support them and the dream succeeds, take part in that joy. In marriage, you share everything. His/her triumphs are also yours.

Michelle & Joseph Lazurek, married 14 years

•••••••••

15. When Jake and I were going through marriage prep, our priest, Father Fillman, advised us to share a meal together daily. Jake and I sit down and eat supper together every night. This week, that has meant supper at the field as they are taking off wheat. (The kids think picnics at the field are fun.) Some days it is the only time we are able to sit and talk. Of course the kids are there too. It allows us to pray, eat, and catch up on our busy and sometimes crazy lives. Our meals create time to communicate with one another. Plus I'm a *great* cook!

Jodi & Jake Griffith, married 8 years

A lot of stay-at-home moms will look at their husbands in the morning and ask, "Are you leaving now?" This is when a husband points out that some 25 million men are leaving their wives right about now.

16. Fifteen years ago we took a premarriage course through our church. One of the pearls of wisdom that we gleaned was to develop a silly catchphrase that would allow a "time-out" of sorts during heated arguments. We did, and it worked! It still works to immediately defuse an intense discussion to this day! And, oh, how we laugh when we throw that phrase out. Instantly we are reminded of why we love each other. We are reminded that winning isn't the endgame. We are reminded that there is grace.

Laughing all the way . . .

—Mark & Missy Pettigrew, married 14 years

17. As a young bride, I was disappointed when the effort of keeping the flame burning seemed to wane with the pressures of everyday life. My husband spent sixty hours every week providing a nice lifestyle, yet I became disillusioned with marriage. I watched many chick flicks and read romance books with fairy tale endings. My actions and expectations were not realistic for everyday life. I now term those days my "season of discontent." My husband could not possibly measure up to the men I was watching or reading about. I learned that the more we keep our minds in the world, the unhappier we will be and the easier it will be for Satan to convince us to give up.

I have been with my husband more than half my life now, and the seasons of discontent have become fewer and fewer. Growing spiritually and making a determined effort to stop comparing our marriage to the world's standards have been crucial elements in finding happiness. The evolution of our marriage now involves aging, more peace, intimacy, friendship, and common ground. We find ourselves enjoying long conversations about the Lord. If there is a void in either of our lives, we pray. There is no perfect person and no one on earth can be everything and all to us like Jesus can. Choose to weather all the seasons of discontent without using the world's measuring stick, and by doing so you will have no seasons of regrets.

—Melanie Davis Porter & Gailen Porter,
married 28 years

Husbands need to learn
two things about PMS:
this too shall pass, and it
will be back next month.

$18.$ We believe a vital key to a happy marriage is to keep things simple between each other. Here are some of those simple things:

- Hold hands whenever you are out in public.
- Kiss and hug—when you wake each morning, when you see each other after being apart, and at the end of the day.
- Laugh, joke, and play with each other.
- Never say words that will intentionally hurt.
- Always desire the best for your partner and encourage him or her to success.

—Marck & Terri Powers, married 5 years

The difference between
a trip and a vacation is
that when you take a
vacation, you leave the
kids at home.

19. We do what we call "emptying our baskets." At the end of each week, we unload everything that's happened to us throughout the week. By doing this, we make sure we aren't drifting away from each other but are in tune with each other's wants/needs/desires and know what's been stressing us out. It's our way to be more a part of each other's lives.

—Chase & Jami Manning, married 9 years

·········

20. Never judge your marriage by the standards of someone else's. And pray you never want a divorce at the same time.

—Heather & Paul Skelton, married 17 years

21. We have both learned that you cannot afford the luxury of taking yourself too seriously. Life is made up of nothing but ups and downs. The key is realizing that the down times will turn around and the up times will stop. So it's important not to be all about yourself.

Whatever happens, be sure to put your spouse first. Make sure you're all there—physically, emotionally, and spiritually—no matter what. Give your total and complete attention to your spouse and the situation at hand. Take time for each other. Make time for each other. Spend time with each other. Then simply ask, "What can I do to make your life better at this time? What is there that I can do to help you right now?"

Then there's the obvious: "Unless the LORD builds the house, the builders labor in vain" (Psalm 127:1). Nothing, I mean nothing, can or ever should take God's place in your marriage!

—Kevin & Cindy Gephart, married 39 years

*Spouses who spent "time alone
with each other, talking, or sharing
an activity" at least once per week
were 3.5 times more likely to be
very happy in their marriage than
spouses who did so less frequently.
So listen to him when he talks
football, and listen to her when she
talks about her mother.

* http://www.nytimes.com/2014/02/15/opinion/sunday/the-
all-or-nothing-marriage.html?_r=0

Husbands, accept that women do need more than food, water, and shelter. Manicures, for instance. Hair coloring. Shoes. Sometimes Botox.

22. My mother told me something early in my marriage I'll never forget. She said, "Trust me when I tell you that love changes. I don't feel the same way about your father as I did when I first met him; it's different and it's better." After twenty-one years of marriage, I finally understand what she meant.

For couples, love begins with intoxicating intensity. All you want to do is be together—nothing else in the world matters. Over time, that intensity diminishes, not because you love each other less, but because the force by which love takes flight cannot be sustained. It reaches cruising speed. Sadly, this is when many people give up. They say things like, "We've grown apart" and "We're both very different people." They begin to mourn what is "lost." They may even find someone else who'll give back to them the high only newness can give.

Oh, the beauty we miss when we pull the roots before they have a chance to take hold. It's astonishing, really. As powerful and indestructible as love is, we have the capacity to alter its course. Had my wife and I allowed ourselves to drift apart, we would have forfeited the joy of our daughters, countless moments together would have never taken place, deep connections with family would have never been known, and the joys and sorrows of life would have never been shared. God's gifts would have been sent back unopened, "return to sender."

Mom told me to stay—don't walk out during the opening scenes. You might miss a beautiful story, so be patient and watch what love will do.

As usual, Mom was right.

—Curt & Polly Harding, married 21 years

23. A strong marriage requires two people who choose to love each other even on the days it's a struggle to like each other.

—Bobby Jo & Scott Kirby, married 10 years

She married you in
spite of your body hair,
but don't be surprised
when she wants you to
shave it off. Draw a line
at waxing.

24. After twenty-three years of marriage, I believe the following to be true:

- I must be careful with my words because while they may be forgiven, they are rarely forgotten.
- My husband does not intuitively know what I want; sometimes I have to tell him.
- Being right isn't so important in the long run.
- You cannot change someone else, but you can change how you react to someone.
- A small kindness goes a long way.
- Not every grievance needs to be discussed. Little things are indeed little.
- The man I married so long ago is the same man I live with today; he will not ever magically transform into Super Hubby, and I can't expect him to.

—Tracy & Steve Line, married 23 years

25. My marriage advice: communicate honestly about all your thoughts and feelings. Always. Don't hold things inside. But while communicating, do it in a way that protects your partner's heart and shows him or her respect. We often feel that our spouse is a good person to unload onto, and we are not careful of their feelings because we think, *this is how I'm feeling right now and they are supposed to love me no matter what.* In actuality, your spouse is the person whose heart you need to protect the most because you two are in your marriage together for a long time.

—Jen Bishop Brockett & Scott Brockett,
married 9 years

26. Within the first year of our marriage, my husband and I moved over 2,500 miles away from the place I had lived my entire life. Less than four years later, we made another journey across the country. Each time we packed our belongings and left behind the town where we had developed roots, we were faced with new challenges.

Over time, we saw that the struggles we were facing were temporary. We realized that God was using each trial to build character and strengthen our faith. With eternal perspective, we knew that each season of our lives, whether joyful or difficult, was part of a larger story God had painted before we ever met. Each stroke became part of the masterpiece—not because of our own ability to create fine works of art, but because God was the painter.

Once we focused on the bigger picture, we were able to face difficulties with a newfound vigor. We knew that no matter what we faced, if we put our trust in God and His provision, He would meet us. We discovered with each twist and turn in our journey that a happy marriage was not something we would simply find. It was a commitment we had to work on each day of our lives.

Sometimes in the midst of trouble, we can only see the turbulence around us and we're tempted to give up, to quit, to throw in the towel. But if we fix our eyes on Jesus, we realize that the trouble we're facing does not compare with the joy of what lies ahead. It's this outlook that will keep us running each leg of the race.

—Abby & Chris McDonald, married 8 years

He thinks that after listening to you talk for ten minutes with the TV on hold, the two of you have now "communicated." After twenty minutes he'll have an elevated heartbeat. Have mercy on him and go call a friend.

27. Our secret was given to us by my mom. Over the years I have written on little slips of paper things I love, appreciate, or like about my husband and put them in a cute little jar. On the days I don't like him so much, or my own mood is making it hard to love him, I take out a slip or as many slips as I need (sometimes the whole jar) to remind myself of all the amazing things I love about him. We have been married thirteen years and counting, so I think it's working so far.

—Charity & Kevin Creech, married 13 years

• • • • • • • •

28. "Let your gentleness be evident to all" (Philippians 4:5). Taking time to process God's advice before spewing harsh words is essential in remembering this simple truth: allowing a smooth, steady stream of gentleness to flow freely is the key to a successful marriage.

—Phil & Kristine Brown, married 20 years

There are times when
a word of encouragement,
instead of the expected
criticism, can save
a marriage.

29. Marsha and I learned the best way to build trust in each other and in our marriage is to be transparent. We do not keep secrets from each other—we have an open door of communication in all areas of our lives. We both have access to each other's cell phones, computers, credit cards, etc. This builds security in our relationship and keeps us closer together.

When decisions need to be made, we make them together. Ever since our sons were young, we have been a united front, a team, so the boys would get the same answer from each of us. Because we share all things, we have a strong bond that cannot be broken.

This closeness in our marriage did not happen right away but has developed over the years. Since we made the decision to care for each other and love each other unconditionally, we've been able to thrive and not just survive. Praying together and praying for each other (which also brings transparency) is a practice we not only preach but is also something we do every day.

Marriage is a wonderful adventure, and caring about your spouse more than you do yourself completes the circle of togetherness.

—Jack & Marsha Countryman, married 50 years

Couples in the longest-lasting marriages agree the wife is always right.

30. Get in the habit of talking to your spouse with uplifting, positive words and genuine compliments. We can get in this habit instead of making negative accusations all the time. Don't let even one rotten word seep out of your mouth. Instead, offer only fresh words that build your spouse up when he or she needs it most. That way your good words will communicate grace to those who hear them.

—Paula & Bill Satterfield, married 39 years,
from *The Voice*

31. Opposites attract. Take the time to figure out what each person needs. If one is an extrovert and one an introvert, there must be an outlet and respect for both needs. If one is organized and the other not, then each should take on responsibilities that they can handle. Knowing what you need for yourself is important. Knowing what your partner needs is important.

—Sarah & Wayne Turbyfield, married 17 years

•·······••

32. Welcome the Holy Spirit into the bedroom. Actively pray together about sexual intimacy in the marriage and watch God bless it.

—Christy & Keith Becker, married 3 years

He's never too old to play football with his friends and come home with a wrenched back and leg cramps. "I told you so" doesn't help here. He needs sympathy.

He won't understand why
you use all those lotions
and creams at night,
but don't be surprised
when he comes to bed
smelling of lilac.

33. During the early days of our marriage we started meeting with four other couples on a weekly basis. At first, our small group met for the purpose of connection and fun and to read and discuss books on marriage. One of the books challenged us to become transparent with other people, specifically about selfishness within our marriage. Talk about some exciting conversations!

In the months that followed, we discovered the power and joy of accountability. Instead of merely reading about "best practices" within marriage, we started asking each other about progress in how we were applying them. Instead of talking about how to serve each other, we challenged and cheered for each other as we actually served our spouses. Something amazing happened as we committed to growth and change in front of other couples and then reported on that change in the weeks ahead.

That's the power of accountability in a marriage. Instead of living in isolation, our small group helped us know and experience deep community.

—Jeff & Lora Helton, coauthors of *The 50 Fridays Marriage Challenge*, married 27 years

Don't be stunned when he comes home with one of your grandmother's fine-linen napkins wrapped around his head like a sweatband. He doesn't understand the purpose of her napkins is to save them, not use them.

34. Stand still and wait on the Lord in peace. Have courage and support each other in love, especially in the love of God. If you wait on Him, He will fight your battles, and your hearts will be filled with His strength.

—Debra & John Barrett, married 32 years

·········

35. I carry a picture of my husband taken when he was about six. The photo reminds me—especially when the grace is running low—that my husband is *first* and foremost God's child and that I have been chosen by God to accompany him on his journey of life. Looking at him as a child usually ushers in a surge of love and appreciation and reminds me that we are all just doing the best we can as we grow up in life . . . and in Christ.

—Toni & Troy Birdsong, married 21 years

36. Two-thirds of communication is listening. God gave us two ears and one mouth.

—Teresa & Tim Barlow, married 18 years

. . . .

37. I recently started moving my clothes into the guest room. I'm not moving out because I don't love my husband, but because I do, and we need to make space in our bedroom for things he needs like a hospital bed and machines that help him breathe, cough, and swallow. Three years ago, he was diagnosed with ALS. Our lives have never been the same, but our marriage has never been stronger. So in order for me to be with him every night, my stuff has to go. The little things I love need to take a back seat for a season so I can focus on the very big thing I love. While this trading in of little for big is not always easy or painless, my deepest regret is that I didn't learn to do it sooner. And my dearest consolation is that it's never too late to start.

—Bo & Steve Stern, married 29 years

When people talk about
communication in marriage,
they mean putting down the
cell phones, the iPads, and
the remote control to listen.
It's hard, especially without
the remote control.

38. Wake up every day thinking what life would be like without your spouse and remember what drew you to him/her in the first place. Don't argue about things that really don't matter because once one of you is gone, the other one will feel terrible for that unimportant bickering.

> —Lelia Sinclair (& Butch) Baldassari,
> married 20 years, widowed 5 years

39. Practice kindness often. Do something for your spouse that you don't necessarily want to do, but do it purely for his or her joy. You may find yourself equally happy.

> —Andrea & Kelly Walker, married 3 years

Here's the difference between husbands and wives: A husband wouldn't dream of touching his wife's clothes. A wife, on the other hand, doesn't think twice about throwing away his clothes she's tired of looking at.

Romance and passion lead to children, which can then lead to the end of romance and passion. Long-lasting marriages figure out how to overcome this.

40. We trust each other's strengths and think of ourselves as a "team." Early on, we determined what tasks we didn't want to do and which ones we did. Both of us cover our share of the household/marriage responsibilities, and we don't argue or stress about it because the decision was made long ago. We don't lie, we respect each other's space when an argument happens, and we pray blessings over each other every night.

—John Turk & Julia Shalom Jordan, married 11 years

•••••••• ••

41. Jay and I never ever talk about issues while we're in bed. That is a sacred place, and we want to keep it that way. We talk about issues in other parts of the house but not in bed or even in our bedroom.

—Jay & Maria Akridge, married 17 years

42. First, don't say no to sex unless you have to (physical ailments and the like). Second, be completely honest with each other. Third, be open to marriage counseling. We can't always communicate to figure things out so we have sought help from godly people who have successful, long marriages. We have taken personality tests and then talked about the results with a counselor. And we also had extensive premarital counseling. That has saved our marriage at times! Fourth, take care of yourself. Whether that means eating well, working out, showering daily, putting on makeup, or just changing out of your yoga pants, make yourself attractive for each other. Maintaining your attraction to each other is important. Last but not least, ask for forgiveness when you've done something hurtful, and forgive, always.

—A'Leah & Randall Knight, married 16 years

43. Laughter . . . not only is it the best medicine, it's also the glue that holds us together. No matter what the circumstance, my husband is always able to make me laugh, which brings everything into perspective. He doesn't have to say anything in particular. I can just look at the little sparkle in his eyes and know that we'll be able to make it through, that we'll come out on the other side better for the experience.

The other key is grace. Remembering that we are all made in God's image, but that we're also human, offering grace is imperative for *both* of you. Grace allows you to overlook some of the irritating little habits, knowing that God has shown us immensely more grace! And for as much grace as you show to your spouse, the same will be shared with you.

—**Kevin & Linda Classen, married 26 years**

When she's pregnant, she might crave cottage cheese with jalapeño peppers and French dressing at two in the morning. Yes, you'll have to get it and bring it to bed. And yes, the smell will keep you up all night.

44. Don't keep your appreciation of your spouse a secret.
I was recently the recipient of an award and asked to give a speech unexpectedly. In the nervous excitement of the moment I thanked everyone I could think of. I thanked friends, family, mentors, and peers. Breathing a deep sigh of relief, I returned to my seat next to my wife. That's when it hit me. *My wife! Oh, no! I forgot to thank my wife! The mother of my children! My biggest supporter and best friend!* Upon that realization, this proud award winner sank in my chair as my stomach did the same.

I spent the ride home uttering a thousand "I'm sorrys" and telling her how much I appreciate her. She was forgiving, but it was that night I realized how important it is not just to tell your spouse how much you appreciate her or him. Tell the world too.

—Matthew & Emily West, married 11 years

•••••••• ••

45. My personal advice as a co-owner with my husband: have goals that you want to reach together. You may arrive at your goals from different directions but you both will be working together.

—Dawn Rose & Barry Floyd, married 16 years

46. Marriage takes three.

—Lee Ann & Tim Sigmon, married 20 years

••••••••••

47. After a few years of marriage, we realized that we did not know how to fight fairly. Our arguments ended up in areas of conflict that had nothing to do with the original problem. So in our prayer time together, the Lord impressed upon my husband to put together what we called a "Fair Fight Covenant." We listed the top ten things that we each did when we were having an argument that weren't fair to the subject matter. For example, bringing in relatives that are "just like *you*" and that is the reason why *you* do the things *you* do. So one of the Fair Fight Covenant agreements was keeping the argument between the two of us and not all of his family or all of mine. We then added a prayer to the bottom of the list and agreed that when we broke one of the agreements, we would stop and ask forgiveness for breaking the covenant. We both signed it and to this day use it as our guide. As pastors, we use this in our premarriage or marriage counseling and it has been very effective for those who adopt the practice.

—Revs. Robert & Martha Horn, married 37 years

Men do not like pimento
cheese sandwiches.
Don't bother asking him.

48. Be the person who replaces the roll of toilet paper. Be the first to say, "I'm sorry." Listen more than you speak. Try to out-love each other. Stay connected sexually.

—Russ & Tonya Stallons, married 21 years

•••••••••

49. Daily maintenance keeps you from having to do major renovations. Own your mistakes. Ask forgiveness and honestly share your feelings and fears with each other. Be real.

—Dave Stone, *Building Family Ties with Faith, Love & Laughter*

Dads never really notice
how kids and dogs smell.
Moms, on the other hand,
keep towels, spray-on
cleaner, handy wipes, and
air freshener within reach
at all times.

50.

1. Fight for and not against each other.
2. Listen to the other person and repeat back what he or she said, even if you don't like or believe what was said. This will cool his or her anger and allow a conversation to commence rather than a fight.
3. When things get too heated, take a thirty-minute break. Anyone can call it; both must respect it. Then come back together and talk it out.
4. Any fights past "the witching hour" should be tabled for the next day. For us this is 11 p.m. Most of the time, the morning brings new light and sanity to the conversation.
5. Give trust to your partner. Distrust breeds distrust and will cause the relationship to die.

—Ruth Well & Russ Crawmer, married 19 years

A pregnant woman
often has a chromosome
that makes her want
to lop off her hair. Tell
her she's beautiful.

51. The number one cause of divorce in America is money fights and money problems. Spouses just don't know how to talk to each other about money. That's because most of the time the husband and wife have totally different personalities about everything—and that includes their money.

In every marriage, there's what I call the Nerd and the Free Spirit. The Nerd has fun with numbers and feels like it gives them control. They feel like they are taking care of their loved ones.

But the Free Spirit doesn't feel cared for; they feel controlled! They don't want anything to do with the numbers, and they tend to "forget" about the budget.

Guess what? Neither the Nerd nor the Free Spirit is "right" or "wrong." You're a team! You need to have a plan, but you need to have some fun. You need to save, but you need to spend a little. The trick is to figure out how your differences can complement each other, and then you can work together.

That only happens when you both sit down together and make a plan.... Both spouses need to have mature input and shared goals.

Larry Burkett used to say that if two people just alike get married, one of you is unnecessary. You and your spouse are different, so celebrate the differences and learn to work together on this money stuff!

—Dave Ramsey, *Total Money Makeover*

Your husband thinks you look perfect. Consequently, he doesn't see the need for $500 a month in cosmetics, Botox, peels, wraps, and a chin lift.

The reason he'll never go on Pinterest is because he likes looking at pictures of cute outfits about as much as she likes standing in a cold river with a fishing pole. Which he loves.

52. What we have learned through thirty years of marriage is you have to be willing to give and take. You won't always be right, and that's okay. A good marriage is always a work in progress. You have to stick with it and love each other through the good times and the bad.

—Diana & Bruce Dunham, married 30 years

....

53. Your spouse should be your *best* friend, but it is important to have other friends.... Don't expect to be all things to each other.

—Mary Main & Steve Nadolson, married 7 years

54. Early in our marriage, we made a decision that every night after work, whenever possible, we would drop everything and spend a cup of coffee's worth of time talking. Sometimes that turned into an hour and dinner was late getting on the table. Sometimes it would get preempted by a child's baseball game or track meet. Much of the time, it was a recap of the day. Time to decompress together and reorient our perspectives. Sometimes it was the prelude to deeper conversation or the opening of an opportunity to talk about things that were troubling us. I really believe that having that time every day—making it a habit—has paved the way for us to keep the walls down and maintain a readiness to communicate. We cherish that time together.

Colette & Paul Varanouskas, married 14 years

....

55. Never compare your spouse with another and express it so that your spouse will feel very little and small. . . . And when you are so angry with him or her, tell God.

Roshini & Dominic Joseph, married 18 years

When she's fighting with her mother, the best thing you can do is get in your car and drive to Nebraska. That's a much better idea than offering your opinion.

56. When we first got married, of course all we saw were the best parts of each other—we could do nothing wrong. Then reality kicked in and, three kids later, his clothes still hadn't made their way to the hamper, my keys never made it to the key holder. With the overwhelming demands of parenthood, everything small seemed super big. At first we just ignored it. I left his clothes where they lay, hoping he'd take notice, but he didn't. Somehow, though, he'd manage to find my keys. Long story short, I finally stopped seeing his clothes on the floor as a nuisance and started seeing them as yet another exercise for trimming my waistline. It worked! This may sound silly, but I stopped feeling irritated about something so small and started seeing and enjoying the beauty in our relationship.

I've come to view our marriage as the union of two people who will *never* have it all together, but will stay together while they enjoy trying.

—Jon & Lisa Seda, married 14 years

Even among the most enlightened
marriages, there is a mom
car and a dad car. The mom
car is where kids eat, play,
spill things, and throw up. The
dad car is where children are
only allowed to breathe—if
they're allowed in at all.

57.

Here are a few things we have learned:
For wives:

1. As with many things in life, God uses marriage as a tool for our sanctification. Marriage will either push you to be more like Christ or show you how far from Him you are.

2. When children come into the picture, it's easy to make them the main focus and priority. But remember that before the kids, all you had was your spouse. One day the kids will leave, and once more all you'll have is your spouse.

3. In the midst of arguments, it's easy for you to feel like you are at the Tower of Babel because no one understands the words that are coming out of your mouth. At those times, stop and pray. And who knows, maybe the Lord can give an interpretation of that tongue.

For husbands:

1. It's easy for the task of breadwinner to become burdensome on the minds of the best of men. But in those times, remember that you are rich not because of how much you have, but because of whom you have: Christ, a godly wife, and/or loving children. Such things are more valuable than all the precious stones.
2. It's probable that the first things that come to our minds when we hear the word *manly* would be descriptions like "strong" or "bold," but life has shown me that the most manly thing you can do in your marriage is be humble.

—Sean & Ruth-Ann Taylor, married 6 years

58. There are many things that keep marriage alive. Date nights, texts, holding hands, and sweet kisses make our hearts melt. A steadfast commitment and a forgiving spirit are the ribbons that tie all those gifts together.

—Carmen & Lary Horne, married 37 years

·········

59. Choose to love. Make the effort to bless your spouse every day, even if it requires super-human strength—in other words, strength from God! Rather than expect perfection from yourself or each other, look for opportunities to extend His grace.

—TJ & Mark Wierenga, married 9 years

The key to intimacy
after having kids is a
lock on your bedroom
door. And Saturday
morning cartoons.

60. I've been happily married sixteen years, and the best insight I've ever heard came just a few years ago during a church liturgy. The priest said, "The purpose of marriage is to help each other get to heaven. The reason marriage doesn't exist in heaven is because you don't need it once you get there."

Wow! What a thought. If only I'd known that when I was a young bride who expected her husband to keep her happy—and blamed him every time she wasn't—I could have saved myself from some pity parties of self-centered frustration.

The longer you're married, the more you realize it's not just about you. It's about your spouse, too, and helping your spouse become the person God designed him or her to be. The best unions are those that chase holiness, not happiness, because only holiness can lead to true happiness. The holier we get, the happier we become.

—Kari & Harry Kampakis, married 16 years

••••••••••

61. Jesus is our first secret! Our other secret is serving each other. We have figured out what blesses the other—serving God and serving each other.

—Rick & Sandra Orwig, married 20 years

You need to remember a crazy mother-in-law is normal for a marriage. Two might be a reason to move overseas.

62.

Early in our marriage, money, or rather the lack of money and budgeting, was a source of tension and conflict. Each time we sat down to discuss something financial we would end up really struggling to understand each other, get frustrated, then walk away. One evening we sat at our small table, Mark at the end and me to his left, and commenced yet another budgeting conversation. And the same scenario began to play again. In the midst of the frustration and conflict I asked Mark if he would move over and sit on the same side of the table next to me so I could see the papers in front of him more clearly. He moved beside me and we returned to the conversation. Amazingly, the entire dynamic changed. The conflict was defused, and we were able to work together to solve the financial situation.

"Sitting on the Same Side of the Table" became a powerful communication tool that night. We learned that when we face a challenge side-by-side, we don't end up tying the problem to one or the other. From that day on we have practiced this, sometimes having to physically get up and sit side-by-side to remind ourselves that the challenge is out in front of us, not between us. Twenty-four years later, it is ingrained in us. It was a tremendously powerful picture to help us become and stay one!

—Sara & Mark Hollis, married 24 years

••••••••••

63. Time is your friend. Not all decisions need to be made today, tomorrow, or even next week. Marriage has ebbs and flows, and by allowing time to work during those periods, hasty decisions and hurtful words that can't be taken back may be avoided.

—Michele & Garth Tennesen, married 40 years

••••••••••

64. I know that a big part of marriage isn't wishing my husband were more like me, but accepting and actually enjoying the fact that he isn't.

—Robin McGraw, *From My Heart to Yours*

••••••••

65. Words that I have shared with many wives: Do you want to be right or do you want to be happy? If we, as women, are more concerned about "winning" every argument, we will end up losing in the end.

— Lisa & Edward Dickerson, married 25 years

If you insist on the
last word, it means
you don't want the
argument to end.

66. Let your spouse be who he is; don't try to change him into you! You fell in love with him or her for a reason. I have learned to stop expecting my husband to do something a certain way because it's how I would do it. His way is just fine and the job still gets done. Just appreciate your differences and learn to work as a team.

—Melissa & Bobby Raymond, married 3 years

Husbands have to
understand that if she
didn't love you, she
wouldn't want to change
everything about you.

Sometimes she'll go
through her closet and
throw out half her
clothes, then announce
she has nothing to wear.
It's a woman thing.

67.

Memorize 1 Corinthians 13.

For Katrina and me, our biggest challenge is Multiple Sclerosis, a disease that renders one of us virtually helpless and the other a caregiver—in my case, a rather unwilling one. But just when I was near a breaking point, I read the biography of someone who studied 1 Corinthians 13—the Love Chapter of the Bible—every day for an entire year.

If I speak in the tongues of men or of angels, but do not have love, I am only a resounding gong....

I decided to do the same; Katrina had already memorized the passage.

Love is patient, love is kind...it is not easily angered....

Living out the Love Chapter is our greatest secret and our biggest joy.

And now these three remain: faith, hope and love. But the greatest of these is love.

—Rob & Katrina Morgan, married 33 years

68. Piece of advice from our wedding day: one good turn gets all the blankets.

On a more serious note, when in dispute, never accuse the other with "you did, you said." Instead, phrase things from your perspective with "I feel . . ." This takes away the blame factor.

—Jacqueline & Robin Gray, married 36 years

....

69. Be willing to do things you wouldn't normally want to do. For example, my husband loves talking about history, particularly war history. I'd rather talk about other things, but the Lord has taught me that as his wife, I'm given the honor to steward this marriage and to love my husband's heart. So I'm learning to invest in his interests and read about what's important to him. Doing this *always* makes him smile. And I think it's a turn-on as well.

—Christy & Keith Becker, married 3 years

If you think your
marriage has lost its
spark after twenty-
five years, try wearing
something other than
flannel pajamas to bed.

70. Never talk negatively about your spouse to others. In our experience, this is something that has helped us tremendously from day one. When you talk negatively about your husband or wife, then:

1. The people you talk to will think negatively of your spouse.
2. It will encourage even more thoughts about your spouse in a bad way (often overexaggerated).
3. It will make it harder to see the good qualities in your spouse.
4. Even after you forgive him or her and move on, others may not have (you have only damaged your spouse's reputation to others).

—Jonathan & Sherilyn Marks, married 4 years

....

71. Faith, hope, and love brought Denise and I together when we most needed it. Each of us wandered without clear purpose or direction for many years. Together we understand we are made whole by showing actions of compassion to others and living to serve. We now live each day to accomplish a mission of servitude to those in spiritual and physical need. Two separated lives may wander hopelessly, but joined in Christ they can create hope and purpose for a world in need of love.

— Roland & Denise Colson, married 5 years

Temptations come and go.
The key is to go, even if
it means going home to
a stressed-out husband
and two children.

72. Strong Christian marriages will still be struck by lightning—sexual temptation, communication problems, frustrations, unrealized expectations—but if the marriages are heavily watered with an unwavering commitment to please God above everything else, the conditions won't be ripe for a devastating fire to follow the lightning strike.

—Gary Thomas, *The Joy of a Sacred Marriage*

73. During a Family Life Marriage Conference, we were advised to never allow two jerks to argue . . . if we felt our spouse was being a jerk, it was our duty to demonstrate maturity and God's grace to the poor soul. Very many times, as the heat began to rise, laughter about maintaining the "jerk count" has replaced my anger. *Plus,* I am reminded to always be kind to the man I chose to spend the rest of my life with.

—Michelle Lee & Dennis Stewart,
married 16 years

74. When we got married, my husband was not a believer and I was not walking with Christ. I made my way back to Jesus about three years in, and he met Jesus face-to-face about five years into the marriage. We have based everything first on our walk with Christ and second on our love for each other. In the twenty-seven years there have been many times that either of us could have (and maybe should have by worldly standards) walked away. But because of our resolve not to let man tear us apart, we have made it through raising three amazing kids and now are reaping the joys of grandchildren together.

God is good. He is faithful. He can redeem anything if you give Him your all. Be patient with God—He's been more than patient with you. Give Him time to change hearts and minds. *Pray* for each other and *pray* for yourself. Be honest in your prayers. God can handle the truth.

—Carla Jo & David Thomas, married 27 years

75. If we expect our marriage to always feel happily ever after, we are in for a rude awakening—like Mary Poppins meets Terminator.

So what do we do? Where do we turn when there's no hope for the perpetual fairy tale? . . .

We need to be careful where we place our hope. Like David, we need to fix our expectations only on the promises of our never-changing, all-loving God. As we do this, we will grow to love and praise Him more and more as we see His faithfulness continually shine through.

Say good-bye to the fairy tale. Put all your hope in the Lord, who is worthy of our trust and who never disappoints!

—**Russ Rice, Brad Silverman & Lisa Guest,**
No Greater Love

If couples never went
to bed angry, the entire
world would be groggy.
The point is to invite
God into the argument
as quickly as possible.

76. Marriage is not a 50%–50% proposition . . . it's a 100%–100% covenant. Both people need to be fully committed to the marriage, to the relationship, to God, and to each other . . . unconditionally . . . forever.

—Kevin & Linda Classen, married 26 years

77. About seventeen years into our marriage, I embraced faith in Jesus and my husband decided he was an atheist. I have learned to love him as Jesus loves him, just as he is and unconditionally—exactly how Jesus loves me. I've learned the importance of being intentional, to stay connected, of not defining my marriage by our faith differences, and to appreciate him every day. Because of this, my husband is one of my greatest blessings in my life. God gave me a marriage that is more than I could have hoped for and more than I could have imagined.

—Dineen & Mike Miller, married 27 years

78. "Oneness" is my word of wisdom. All happiness in marriage comes when a couple achieves oneness. The only way to achieve oneness is to become a student of your spouse and serve him or her the way that Christ served the church—selflessly. When you strive to serve your spouse the way that Christ served the church, then you will slowly begin to learn everything about them, what makes them special to you, and how to make them feel special. When you are able to make them feel special, you will have endless love, joy, fun, and excitement in your marriage. The important thing to remember is, this takes time. Your spouse doesn't think like you do so ask questions to learn about him or her. Don't just assume you know what they want because you will probably be wrong. Ask, listen, and learn, and you can achieve oneness.

—Matt & Denise Buffum, married 30 years

*According to the *New York Times*, the more a husband cooks and cleans, the more a wife loves him, but the less she is attracted to him sexually. Even women can't figure this out.

* http://www.nytimes.com/2014/02/09/magazine/does-a-more-equal-marriage-mean-less-sex.html

79.

- Never talk badly about your spouse in public. This has to be a serious commitment for both of you.
- Be respectful of each other. Just because you're married doesn't mean you let go of all restraint and say whatever pops into your head. Words are impossible to take back.
- Be a team—not opponents.
- Find another great couple to be marriage mentors.
- Counseling can help *any* couple.
- Date your spouse.
- Assume the best of intentions from each other.
- Pick your battles.

—Rebecca & Ron Gore, married 13 years

80. We believe it is important for your spouse to know how much you appreciate him or her and sometimes your spouse needs to be reminded. "Thank you" goes a long way even in a marriage. Don't take for granted the things your spouse does for you on a regular basis. Show him or her how much you care by doing the little things that matter most.

—Candace & Darnell Smith, married 5 years

81. Aside from keeping Jesus as a center point, our "secret" is just to *be* there for each other. Don't blame. Don't judge. Don't nag or argue, sometimes don't even discuss. When one is having a down time, don't rub in your "up," but try to bring the other up.

—Karen & Leigh Fahel, married 28 years

He'll expect generous praise
when he changes the
light bulbs. If he actually
repairs the disposal without
calling a plumber, he'll
expect to be treated like it
is your wedding night.

82. We went to a Weekend to Remember retreat, and one of the best things we took away from it was to look at each other and say "You are *not* my enemy!" It was such a huge reminder that Satan is constantly working on breaking up the family, which is one of God's beautiful creations that the world can see.

—Wendy & Terry Howes, married 11 years

....

83. We recently went through a hard five-year stint of illness, tragedy, and heartache which took its toll on our relationship. Finding our way back to each other was hard work, but being in the moment and focusing on each other was the key. Rediscovering each other's wants, needs, and desires all over again has made us appreciate each other even more.

—Jim & Patty Venneman, married 26 years

Don't be shocked if you bring home a Porsche and she orders you to send it back. Wives just don't understand.

If you haven't shaved
in five days, don't be
surprised when she
won't let you touch her
at night unless you get
up and shave.

84. "Husbands, love your wives, just as Christ loved the church and gave himself for her" (Ephesians 5:25 HCSB).

Sometimes I feel that verse could just as easily read, "Husbands, *learn* your wives." Maybe a commitment to learning is really the only way to love. I know I've had to learn my wife. I'll explain.

Jennifer is gentle and kind; in other words, very sensitive. That's who God created her to be. If she were different, she wouldn't be Jennifer. So I've had to learn to be gentle and kind with her. Now that's not who I naturally am; I have a tendency to, well, not be so gentle or kind at times. But if I'm serious about loving Jennifer—and I am—then I'll set aside my natural tendencies and seek to love her as she's been created. It's what that verse means when it says "gave Himself for her."

So, husbands, don't claim to love your wife if you're not willing to learn her. Your claims won't be believable to those around you or, most important of all, to your wife. Jesus is our example in this: He knows us, and He loves us.

—Josh Turner, *Man Stuff*

85. The glue that continues to hold our marriage together is our faith in God. We have chosen to make Him the center of everything we do. He is the third strand of our triple-braided matrimony cord, not easily broken (Ecclesiastes 4:12). With Him, we have everything we need for our marriage to thrive!

—Keith & Leah DiPascal, married 28 years

•••••••••

86. Love is a choice that you will have many opportunities to put into practice. Do one thing nice for your partner even if you don't feel like it—something above the ordinary. Life, even in marriage, is about change. Growing together is about how you respond to those changes.

—Mike & Donna Coman, married 33 years

After about the tenth
anniversary, she no
longer wants sexy
underwear. She wants
comfortable pajamas.

87. When we married, we did not have solid role models from which to draw, so we turned to the one source we knew would provide the best direction and wisdom for marriage—the Bible. Our commitment to Christ translated to a commitment to each other and our marriage. In difficult times, we have clung to our commitment made before God above the temptation to end our marriage.

—Mark & Jonnie Gomez, married 35 years

He won't understand your
need to continually update
your wardrobe. His suits are
twenty years old. His ties
could be thirty. His T-shirts
are falling apart. He's happy
with his look.

88. Marital harmony exists when two people resolve to "make every effort to keep the unity of the Spirit" (Ephesians 4:3). Here are some ideas:

Be considerate. "Husbands, in the same way be considerate as you live with your wives" (1 Peter 3:7). The word *consider* shares ancestry with the word *knowledge*. It means to "have an understanding of." The wise thing is to be considerate of your husband, or your wife.

Love "does not demand its own way" (1 Corinthians 13:5 NLT). Don't try to change your mate. Don't change the "I do" into an "I'll redo." Meet in the middle. Be flexible. Yield your rights. Give and take. Learn the art of negotiation. Compromise.

Keep courting. What you did to fall in love, keep doing so you'll stay in love. "May you rejoice in the wife of your youth" (Proverbs 5:18). "Enjoy life with your wife, whom you love" (Ecclesiastes 9:9). Enjoy your spouse. Encourage each other. If there was more courting in marriage, there would be fewer marriages in court.

Fight fairly. Never criticize your spouse in public. Don't hide stones in snowballs. Don't harbor grudges or dredge up the past. When a fight starts, be quick to listen and slow to speak. Honor each other.

Lock the escape hatch. Throw away the key. Commitment is what makes a marriage great. No matter how angry you are and how much you may hate that person at the moment, you do not bring up the subject of divorce, because it's not even an option.

Love Christ even more than you love each other. When the husband focuses on growing toward Christ and the wife focuses on growing toward Christ, it automatically brings them together. Christ is not going to fight with Christ.

—Max Lucado, *Max on Life*

89. Ephesians 4:26 reminds us, "Do not let the sun go down while you are still angry." Beth and I have tried to live by that verse. When something's wrong, we talk it out, and we don't go to bed until it's settled.

The priniciple has worked quite well for us, although there was that one time we stayed up for two weeks . . .

It's a good rule to live by.

—Dave Stone, *Building Family Ties with Faith, Love & Laughter*

·•·•·••

90. We both came from broken homes where communication wasn't a priority between our parents. After getting engaged, we determined that communication was going to be a major building block in our marriage. We talk about everything, no matter how embarrassing, painful, or seemingly insignificant.

Also, when going to premarital counseling, our pastor gave us this piece of advice: always give 100% and expect 0%.

—Elmer & Terri Jones, married 26 years

She will think you'd rather
be with your friends than
with her just because
you're going to a football
game with them rather
than shopping with her.
Here, you must lie.

91. Oftentimes, we look to our spouse for identity and fulfillment. True and lasting fulfillment comes only from Jesus. When I learned that truth and began living it and seeking Jesus to fulfill my needs, I started to become the wife my husband needed. Jesus has to be Lord of my life—when I am filled with Him, then I am better able to love my husband the way God intended.

—Aimee & Marcus Imbeau, married 16 years

92. My husband once preached a sermon series (and wrote a book) called *Moral Earthquakes*. His premise was this: earthquakes don't just happen. Instead, they are caused by things beyond our sight, well beneath the surface of the ground. Earthquakes are preceded by a series of small seismic movements along the fault lines that have been building for many years.

This truth is particularly applicable to marriage. Small fault lines can so easily develop in our hearts if we aren't vigilant. Failure to forgive, resentment, dwelling on our spouse's weaknesses, unresolved anger, and many other negatives can create fault lines that may eventually erupt into an earthquake. Marriages don't fall apart overnight, but reach that point gradually. What to do? Diligently work through your issues together, resolve to forgive, believe the best of each other, and move forward. This, we believe, is the key to a good marriage!

—Susie & O. S. Hawkins, married 44 years

All wives need to remember one simple fact: men are not mind readers. You need to tell him what you are thinking.

93. "Let all bitterness, wrath, anger, clamor, and evil speaking be put away from you, with all malice. And be kind to one another, tenderhearted, forgiving one another, even as God in Christ forgave you."

—Ephesians 4:31-32 NKJV

....

94. Sandy and I were married for nine years ending in divorce. After seven years of divorce, God healed our broken marriage, and since then we have been together for thirty-one years. Our wisdom for a happy marriage is: pray together. Always pray.

—Walter & Sandy Fox, married 40 years

Wise husbands stay
as far away as they
can from mother-
daughter issues.

95.

We were high school sweethearts who married very young at ages eighteen and nineteen. Our pastor provided pre-marriage counseling to us, and we've found that this principle has been a lasting foundation for our marriage: he said that when we argue (we couldn't believe we'd *ever* argue about *anything*!), to remember that we're on the same team. Team members don't face each other, they stand shoulder-to-shoulder to face a common enemy. For the past thirty-two years, we have faced many enemies: illnesses, joblessness, financial ruin, babies, toddlers, teenagers in rebellion, the deaths of loved ones, and our son's repeated deployments to Iraq during the worst possible times of war there. From the beginning, we made the resolute decision that Jesus Christ was going to be in the center of our marriage, and through all of the difficult times, the heartaches, and trials, God has been our anchor. We have endured because we've stood shoulder-to-shoulder with each other and aligned ourselves with God's Word and His promises. Marriage is a partnership, a team sport. It requires that we trust that each person will do what it takes to make the team successful.

—Bill & Jeanne Bolt, married 32 years

96. Marriage is like a car. A car needs to have periodic maintenance to keep running. So does a marriage. It is work. We have had to work hard to maintain friendship, companionship, loyalty, and love. These qualities don't just happen, they are intentional. Never give up, never give in, and never look back. Yesterday is gone, today is a blink, and tomorrow may not arrive.

—Michael & Sheila Van Dyke, married 33 years

•••••••••

97. Never forget the person you married and why you married him or her. Strive to be that same person your partner married—fun, loving, exciting—and make time to be those same two people who fell in love.

—Charla & David Bennett, married 21 years

There's a real chance she
wants to do something
else than play *Grand
Theft Auto* with you all
night. Um, ask her.

98. Marriage takes a lot of dedication and devotion. You really change throughout the years, and so does your spouse. The trick is to keep changing and going in the same direction, and to keep your eyes on Jesus. Never stop talking to each other, and try to carve out time for each other as much as possible. Always respect your spouse and never, ever, talk behind his or her back in a negative way. This is old-fashioned advice, but it is tried and true!

—Mitch & Karee Kopyto, married 29 years

· · · · · · · · · ·

99. I have learned that love is not an emotion, but rather a choice. Both people have to wake up every day and *choose* to love and respect each other. You make that agreement and commitment up front and literally wake up and say, "No matter what happens today, I will choose to love, respect, and honor my spouse."

—Cheryl & Chris McNabb, married 22 years

It's an established fact that
married men tend to live
longer, though they lose
more sleep, spend more
money, and work longer
than their single brothers.

100. "Put on love, which is the bond of perfection."

—Colossians 3:14 NKJV

· · · · · · · · ·

101. The secret to a happy marriage for us was when we realized how important it is to embrace marriage as a journey—both the good moments and the more challenging ones. Every action and reaction we share as husband and wife, every moment we experience in marriage is a brushstroke of colorful paint smeared across the canvas of life. We are creating a beautiful masterpiece of art, of love, of marriage. Every shade of color is valuable, the dark and the light, every moment we encounter, every tear, and every laugh.

Marriage is a beautiful journey.

—Aaron & Jennifer Smith, author of
The Unveiled Wife, married 7 years

The trick to a successful
marriage is falling
in love over and over
again. Even if he's
fallen asleep holding
the remote control.

Proverbs 31
MINISTRIES

If you are a woman who wants to strengthen your marriage and deepen your personal relationship with Jesus Christ, we encourage you to connect with Proverbs 31 Ministries.

The women at Proverbs 31 Ministries exist to be trusted friends who will take you by the hand and walk by your side, leading you one step closer to the heart of God through their:

- Online Bible studies
- Daily radio program
- Books and resources
- *Encouragement for Today* devotions

For more information about Proverbs 31 Ministries,
visit: www.Proverbs31.org.

Harry H. Harrison, Jr. is a nationally acclaimed author appearing on the *NY Times* and *Booksense* lists. He has over 3.6 million books in print featuring titles such as *Father to Son, Father to Daughter, 1001 Things Happy Couples Know about Marriage,* and more. He and his wife, Melissa, have been married 43 years.